365 Days of Art

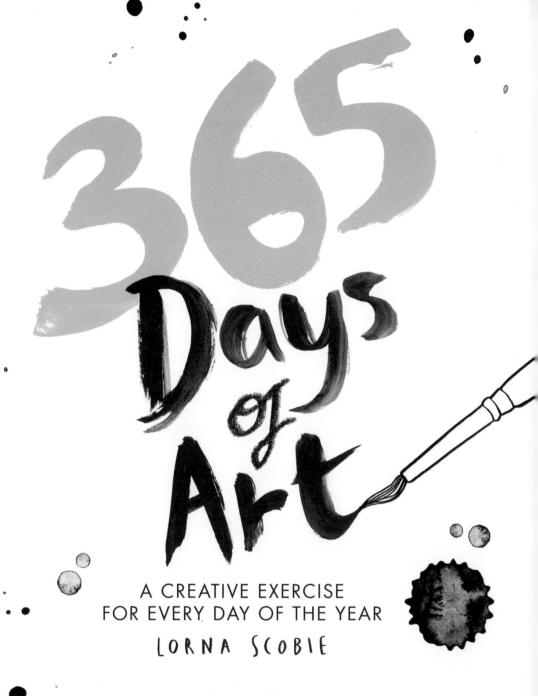

365 Days of Art

A CREATIVE EXERCISE
FOR EVERY DAY OF THE YEAR

LORNA SCOBIE

Hardie Grant

BOOKS

Welcome to 365 Days of Art!

The purpose of this book is to discover and rekindle a love of art by embarking on a creative project every day. This is a book for anyone who has a desire to create: whether you have a passion for drawing, but can never find the time to do it, you feel too intimidated (or busy!) to take part in a class or are simply just unsure of where to start. *365 Days of Art* helps you to nurture your creative skills in a journal that you can keep as a record of your progress.

To conquer the intimidating prospect of filling 365 blank spaces, I've started a lot of the projects off for you. I have also tried to vary the activities, to help you learn different artistic skills and encourage you to experiment with many artistic mediums. Practise your penmanship with the calligraphy tutorials, or for something a little more relaxed, create colour wheels and explore the varying textures of paint, pencil, charcoal and pastel crayons.

Although the activities are numbered, you can approach them in any order you like – just choose one that suits you at the time. Drawing doesn't have to be complicated or intimidating; it just requires practice. I have created some activities that look at specific skills such as approaches to using light and shade, observing perspective or learning how to draw a face. By practising these skills you'll soon be able to transfer them to bigger artworks of your own and unearth a depth of artistic talent you never knew you had!

Finding the time to draw can be difficult. There's always an excuse not to: after-work socials or staying back late to meet a deadline make it difficult to squeeze in some art therapy. Or for those nights you do make it home on time, it just seems easier to turn on the TV and tune into the latest series. I am not going to lie: a little discipline is needed! But I find that as soon as I start drawing and getting creative, it becomes easier and more enjoyable. I love painting to my favourite tunes or listening to a podcast. If you can't bring yourself to have a totally television-free night, even switching on a calming nature documentary can become a stimulating backdrop to your creative exploration.

Drawing can be incredibly relaxing and good for the mind, and even spending as little as 10 minutes a day on a little sketch or colouring-in, can help ease regular daily tensions. Be mindful by considering the colours you choose and the marks you make and allow yourself to get lost in your art. Think of it as a relaxing bubble bath for your mind; a time to de-stress, unwind and switch off from everything else.

Time spent being creative is never time wasted: sometimes it's simply the thought of picking up the pen and making that first mark that can feel like the hardest part! But don't let that stop you. I've found that drawing every day has helped me feel less worried about getting started, as well as feeling less intimidated about 'getting it wrong'. If a drawing doesn't work out today, it's fine: I can try another approach tomorrow.

As well as art activities, there are helpful tips to help build your artistic confidence. There aren't any rules in this book, just suggestions,

so feel free to adapt the activities however you wish. Perhaps you'd prefer to use a different material to the one suggested – that's fine! This is your book. The great thing about art is that there isn't a right or wrong answer, because it's all about personal expression. Develop your own style of working by using the materials you love and remember that the process of creating is as important as the final creation.

Don't feel pressure to complete an activity every single day. There is a year's worth of art activities here, but feel free to spread them out over a longer period, or just dip in when you feel compelled to create. The most important part of these creative tasks is that you enjoy yourself and as time goes on, you will find an artistic style that works for you. I really hope that you will become inspired to continue your creative journey beyond this book. I encourage you to explore, take risks and make mistakes – but most of all, have fun!

Your creations can be personal and private, but if you'd like to share them, do so with confidence! Use the hashtag **#365DaysOfArt** to share your art with the online community.

Activities Completed

X	2	3	4	5	6	7	8	9	10
11	12	13	14	15	16	17	18	19	20
21	22	23	24	25	26	27	28	29	30
31	32	33	34	35	36	37	38	39	40
41	42	43	44	45	46	47	48	49	50
51	52	53	54	55	56	57	58	59	60
61	62	63	64	65	66	67	68	69	70
71	72	73	74	75	76	77	78	79	80
81	82	83	84	85	86	87	88	89	90
91	92	93	94	95	96	97	98	99	100
101	102	103	104	105	106	107	108	109	110
111	112	113	114	115	116	117	118	119	120
121	122	123	124	125	126	127	128	129	130
131	132	133	134	135	136	137	138	139	140
141	142	143	144	145	146	147	148	149	150
151	152	153	154	155	156	157	158	159	160
161	162	163	164	165	166	167	168	169	170
171	172	173	174	175	176	177	178	179	180

181	182	183	184	185	186	187	188	189	190
191	192	193	194	195	196	197	198	199	200
201	202	203	204	205	206	207	208	209	210
211	212	213	214	215	216	217	218	219	220
221	222	223	224	225	226	227	228	229	230
231	232	233	234	235	236	237	238	239	240
241	242	243	244	245	246	247	248	249	250
251	252	253	254	255	256	257	258	259	260
261	262	263	264	265	266	267	268	269	270
271	272	273	274	275	276	277	278	279	280
281	282	283	284	285	286	287	288	289	290
291	292	293	294	295	296	297	298	299	300
301	302	303	304	305	306	307	308	309	310
311	312	313	314	315	316	317	318	319	320
321	322	323	324	325	326	327	328	329	330
331	332	333	334	335	336	337	338	339	340
341	342	343	344	345	346	347	348	349	350
351	352	353	354	355	356	357	358	359	360
361	362	363	364	365					

Materials

There are so many different materials that can be used to create art. Finding a set of materials that you enjoy using will be a constantly developing journey as you try new tools and experiment. You don't need to have the perfect materials or a complete set straight away – enjoy building your collection over time, and remember that you can create equally amazing art with a simple ballpoint pen as you can with an expensive set of acrylics.

Art and craft shops will stock high-quality and sometimes very niche materials. Here you can browse at leisure, try out materials and ask for recommendations and advice. Stationery shops also have a broad range of cheaper (but still excellent) materials, including pencils and pens. You can also find materials online, where reviews and comments can help you decide which products are right for you.

Here are some of my own personal favourites, but you can of course use anything you prefer:

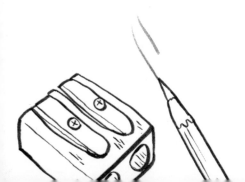

Pencils

Any standard wooden pencil should do the job! Pencils range in softness, most commonly from a 9B, which will create a very soft black line, to a 9H, which is very hard and creates a very sharp, light line. It might be useful to have a variety of pencils so you can experiment with the different effects they make. Try a 2B for shading and an H or 2H for delicate, fine lines.

You could also try a mechanical pencil. Despite still containing a pencil lead, these feel more like you are holding a pen, and often have a rubber grip for your fingers. I enjoy using the Staedtler Mars Micro 0.5, and the Pentel P205 0.5. Mechanical pencils don't need sharpening, but you will need to buy extra lead for them. Make sure you choose the correct size of lead for your pencil. (The mechanical pencil will say what lead it takes on its side.)

A good eraser and pencil sharpener make perfect companions for your pencils.

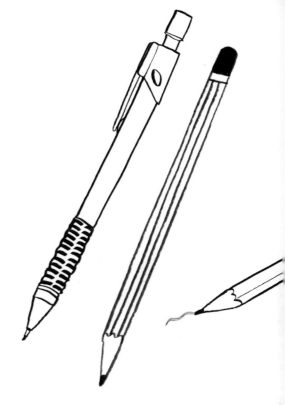

Fineliner Pens

It's really useful to have a few black pens in your kit. These can be used for anything from jotting down notes and ideas, to quick sketches and adding details to artwork. There is a wide range of brands and nib sizes to choose from, so I recommend experimenting with the testers in an art store to see which you prefer. My favourites include the Uni Pin Fine Line pens, the Pigma Micron pens and the Derwent Graphik Line Maker pens, but there are plenty more to choose from.

Coloured Pencils

Coloured pencils are a quick, easy and mess-free material. My favourite sets are the Staedtler Ergosoft pencils, which are hard and create very solid, bright colour, and the Caran d'Ache Supracolor pencils, which have a softer lead and come in a huge range of colours. Some coloured pencils are water-soluble, so you can blend them with a damp paint brush to add extra dimension to your work.

If you are looking for specific colours, you can also purchase coloured pencils on their own in art shops. I find it very handy to have some extra black, brown and grey pencils as I use these colours a lot. The Faber-Castell Polychromos pencils last a long time and produce a lovely strong colour.

Watercolour Paints

Sizes of watercolour palettes can vary. It's convenient to have more colours in your palette, but the smaller sets are also great and you can blend to create a whole rainbow of shades. Daler Rowney and Winsor & Newton both produce wonderfully vibrant colours. When you run out of a particular colour, you can even purchase individual replacements so your set of watercolours can last forever!

Paint brushes vary greatly too, and it's useful to have a range of brush sizes and shapes. Tips can be pointed, rounded and even flat, and each will produce a different effect. Experiment with different types. You'll also need a container for your water, which can be anything from a mug to an old cut-up carton, and some paper towel for blotting water off your brush. Make sure your brush is wet before you use it to pick up watercolour paint, and clean it in the water before changing colour to keep colours bright.

Tip: You don't have to apply paint with brushes. Try using pieces of card, sticks and even flowers!

Brush Pens

These are essential for calligraphy. You can use a pot of black ink and a paint brush for brush lettering, but it can get a little messy! I really enjoy using brush pens with a cartridge of ink inside that can be replaced. Be careful as they can dry out quickly, but they are a great alternative to brushes and ink pots because they are so easy to use and the ink stays relatively contained. I like the Pentel Brush Pen but there are plenty of others available, and some even come with coloured ink cartridges.

Coloured paper

Coloured paper and origami paper can be purchased from art and stationery shops, but you could also collect different colours and textures over time. A stockpile of paper, whether from magazines, brown paper or wrapping paper, could come in handy for a collage, or be used as a background of a drawing.

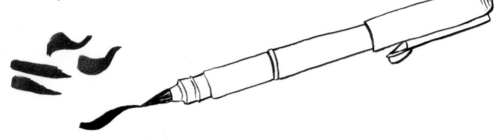

Here are some other materials that might be handy for your basic kit:

— **Sketchbooks:** You may find you'd like to continue creating outside of this book. Sketchbooks can be a visual diary, where you should feel comfortable to experiment and make mistakes as well as potentially create some amazing artwork!

— **A good pair of scissors:** For collages and cutting shapes and stencils.

— **PVA glue:** For sticking down paper and collected objects. This can be watered down to make it less gloopy.

— **Water brush pens:** These brushes can be filled with water and provide a useful alternative to a pot of water and paint brush when painting with watercolours.

— **Masking tape (sticky tape):** Handy for sticking down things quickly, and easy to remove and draw on.

— **Tracing paper:** You can use masking tape to stick tracing paper over messy drawings to protect them.

— **Charcoal:** A wonderful medium to explore tone and shadow.

— **Oil pastels:** Can be smudged with your fingers to blend colours.

— **Acrylic paint:** Strong, bright colours, which dry quickly and can also be watered down. Be sure to wash brushes before the paint on them dries.

— **White china marker:** For adding white highlights to drawings.

1 ——————— Colour or create a pattern.

3 ——————— When drawing outside, you could choose to focus on particular elements of a building – perhaps the shape of the rooftops, or the edge of a building against the blue sky. Add your own building to the sky on the next page.

Tip: Select areas to draw that interest you.

4 ———————— Fill the page with swatches of colour.

5 ———————— Colour in the fruit, but try not to use the correct colours.
Challenge your mind.

6 —————— Complete the shoal of colourful fish.

7 —————— Draw someone you know from memory.

8 —————— Draw a collection of vegetables.

9

Continue to add details to the feathers and the leaves using line.

10

Experiment with different materials to discover what you enjoy using. Today, use a chubby pencil crayon to create different marks. As they are so thick and waxy, they are more difficult to control than regular coloured pencils.

Tip: Chubby pencil crayons can produce fun results, but are also messy. To protect the opposite page, you could attach a layer of tracing paper to this page, once you have finished.

11 ———————— Practise drawing the features on the faces here.
Draw the eyes about halfway down the face.

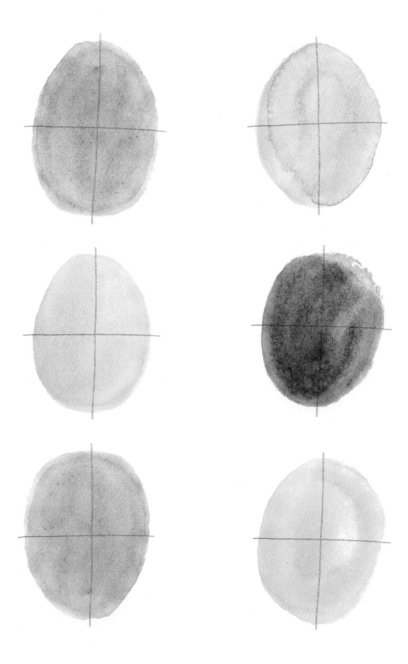

—————— Add leaves and fruit to the branches of the tree.

13 ——— Colour the white circles to create different colour combinations. Perhaps you will find a new colour pairing which you haven't considered before. Does the colour look appealing against the background stripe?

14 ———— Fill this section with flowers.

15 ———— Find a pattern that inspires you. It could be in a magazine, on paper, or fabric. Stick it here if you can, or draw it.

16

Begin learning how to create calligraphy today, with a brush pen (or paint brush and ink). A brush pen can be used in different ways to create varying types of stroke. A 'stroke' is the mark made by the brush. The basic idea for calligraphy is that when you are moving the brush down the paper, you use a thick, 'full' stroke. When you move the brush up the page, use a thinner stroke. Practise making the different strokes below.

Full stroke: Put pressure on your pen, pushing the brush down towards the paper, and drag downwards to create a full stroke.

A lot of the side of the brush has contact with the paper.

Thin stroke: Use the tip of the brush to create a thin line when moving upwards. You don't need much pressure, and you may have to practise keeping your hand steady.

You may find it easier to hold the brush at a steeper angle.

Full stroke to thin stroke: Now, try combining the two strokes by relieving the pressure once you start to turn the corner. The trick is to start to lift the pressure slightly before you turn the brush. Start by moving down the page with a full stroke, then slowly move into a thin stroke as you move upwards.

Relieve pressure here.

Tip: Remember to adjust the angle at which you hold your brush as you move from full to thin stroke.

17 ———— Fill the page with loops. Try different colours.

18 ———— Colour in the fish.

Design a wallpaper behind this chair.

20 ———— Design your own fairy (twinkle) lights.

21 ———— What is your favourite simple thing to eat?
Draw or write it here.

22 ———— What made you smile today? Draw or write it here.

23 ———— Fill the page with coloured dots.

24 ———— Colour in the stripes.

25 ———— Fill the squares with different marks. You could try dashes, lines, spots, swirls and crosshatches.

Add your own scene to this river. Perhaps there are people or animals along the bank? Is the river in a jungle? The countryside? Or a city?

Continue creating your own patterns. Select warm colours.

Design some T-shirts.

Explore colours that look good together. Fill in the boxes with colours that you think work well side by side.

30

Add details to these flowers. You could use cut-out pieces of paper, or any other material you like.

31

Draw your desk or a table, using any materials you feel like. Perhaps you will draw the table itself, or what you see on top of it.

32

Add foliage to the rest of the trees. Perhaps you could draw the individual leaves, or use a more abstract shape to suggest the form of the tree.

33 ———————— Draw a page of stars in any style you like.

34 —————— Continue practising calligraphy by using this page to explore mark making. Over time, your confidence using a brush pen should build.

Tip: Explore how using the brush pen quickly or slowly can change the amount of ink transferred onto the page.

35 ——— Complete the pattern.

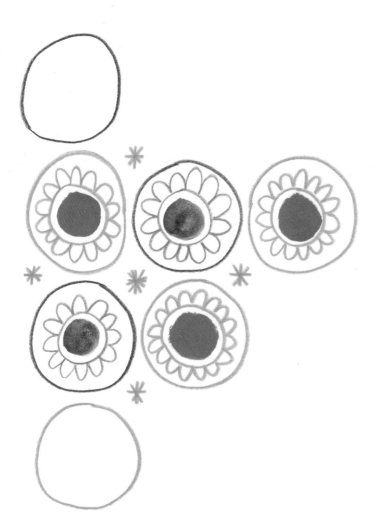

————— Paint the ocean from your imagination.

37

Fill a page with things that are the colour red.

38 ——— Draw within the black areas using white pastel or a chalky white coloured pencil.

39 ———— Draw a pair of glasses or sunglasses.

40 ———— Open a picture book, turn to a page at random and draw something from that page.

41 ——— Create a flock of birds of paradise by adding wings, tail feathers, beaks and legs.

42 ——————— Sometimes, when you are stuck for creativity, it's useful to draw something you love. It could be a 'thing', a person, an animal, a plant – anything.

43 ——————— Conversations can be the start of stories and ideas. Write down an interesting conversation that you have heard.

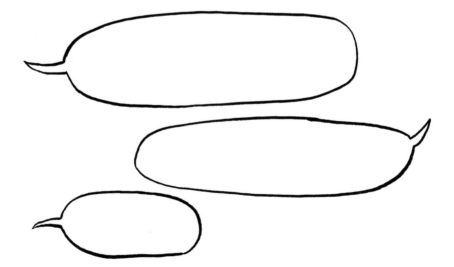

44 ———— Colour in the plants.

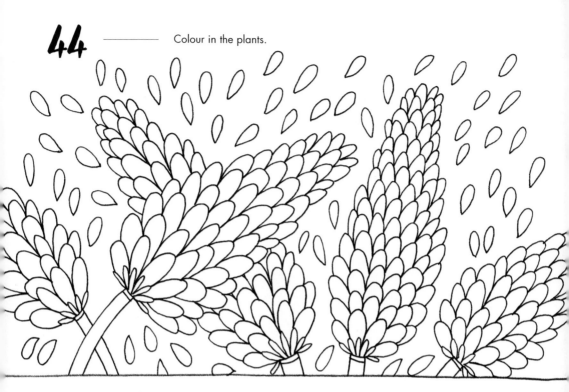

45 ———— What activities make you feel relaxed?
Draw or write it here.

46

There are lots of ways to create an image – you don't have to draw with a pencil. Try a collage today. Choose some objects, or a scene. Observe the shapes, then cut or tear paper to create a simple still life. Keep adding layers of paper until you are happy, then add details in pencil as a contrast to the block shapes.

Tip: Before you stick it down, you can move the paper around your page until you are happy with the composition. If you don't have the right coloured paper, you can use coloured pencil to colour onto paper, before you cut or rip your shapes.

47 ——————— Fill the page with coloured stripes.

48

Calligraphy practice: use the brush pen to practise moving from thin to full strokes by drawing rings. Start at the top using a thin stroke, then move the brush down and around, applying more pressure as you do. Once at the bottom, return to the top and do the same on the other side to complete the ring.

Start with a thin stroke here.

Apply more pressure.

O O O O O

Relieve pressure here.

Apply pressure again.

49 ——— Add your own colourful flowers to the vines.

50

Design a pattern using the grid.

———— Add patterns to the vases.

Continue the pattern.

Add trees to the forest.

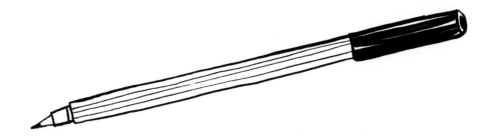

Fill the bowl with a mixture of colourful fresh fruit.

57

Colour in the concentric circles. These could be shades of different colours such as purple or blue. Consider what moods these colours might represent – perhaps calmness or serenity.

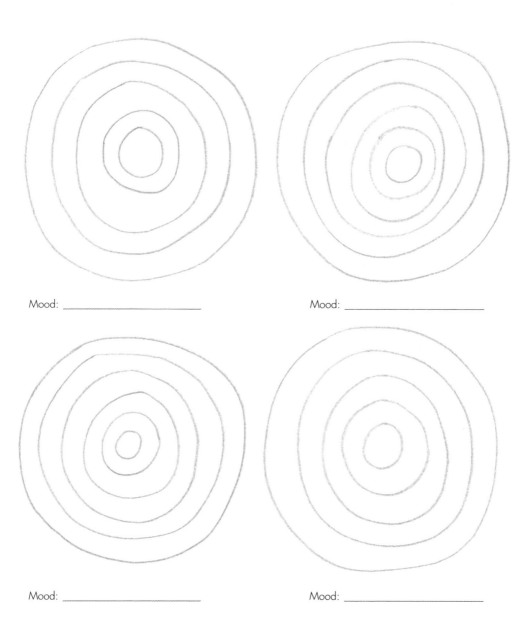

Mood: _____

Mood: _____

Mood: _____

Mood: _____

Design a T-shirt.

59 —————— Fill a page with things that are the colour yellow.

—————— Colour in the dots.

61

Calligraphy practice: use a brush pen to practise thin to thick lines. Start at the top using a thin line, then move the brush down, applying more pressure as you do. Keep your shoulder loose and relaxed.

Bring the brush down using a full stroke.

Start with a thin stroke here.

Relieve pressure here to form a thinner stroke.

62 ———————— Colour in the waves.

63 ——— Fill the opposite page with textures and mark making. Explore the materials you have. Try using paints with both wet and dry brushes.

Continue to add flowers to the meadow.

65

Calligraphy practice: practise joining full strokes and thin strokes to make 'u' shapes.

Bring the brush down and around using a full stroke.

As you bring the brush up, use a thin stroke.

Fill the squares with different marks.

Complete the pattern.

68 ———————— Using a black fineliner, draw your hand. I suggest you draw the hand that is drawing. Start by drawing the nib of the pen, then work up.

Tip: This is difficult, but worth practising. Look carefully and draw what you see, not what you expect to see.

69 ———— Continue creating your own patterns. Select cool,
calming colours.

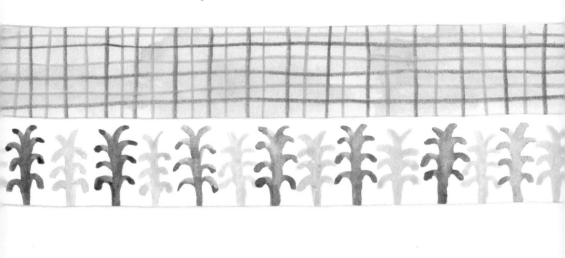

70

Experiment with different art materials to discover what you enjoy using. Today, use coloured pencils to create different marks. Try using the side of the nib to create broader lines, and blending different colours. Applying more or less pressure can change the intensity of the colour.

Add shadows to the glass bottles. Try different ways of drawing them.

72 ——————— Colour in or design a pattern.

73 ——————— Add trees to this half page.

74 ——————— Draw the weather today.

75 ——————— Draw something from nature that you've seen today.

76 ——————— Draw an object using coloured pencils or pastels. Use this coloured background as a mid-tone. Use light colours to draw the highlights and darker colours to draw the shadows.

Explore colours that look good together. Fill in the boxes with colours that you think work well as a group.

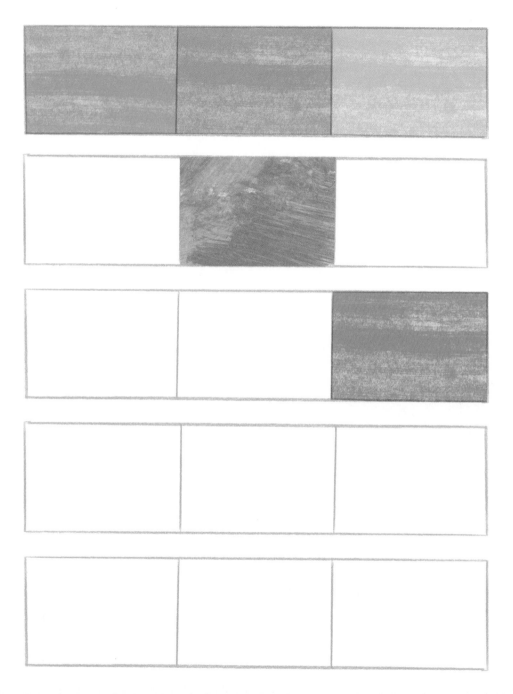

78 ———— Design the Dala horses.

79 ———— Conversations can be the start of stories and ideas. Write down an interesting conversation that you have heard.

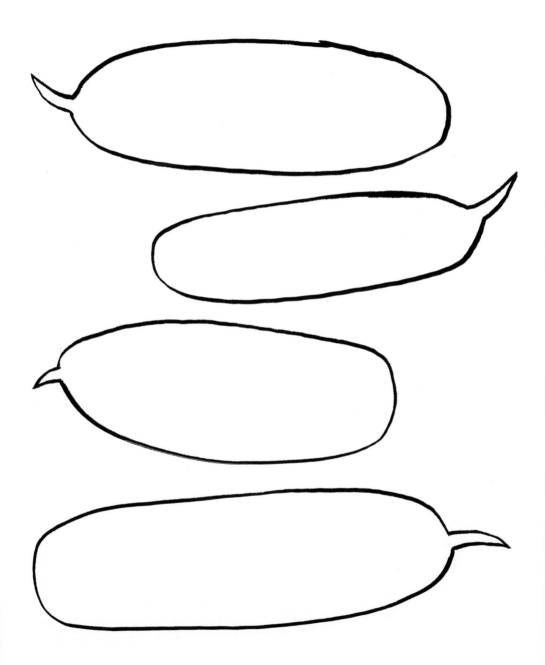

80

Today, draw an object, but this time, hold your pencil in the opposite hand to the one you normally use. If you are left-handed, use your right hand. If you are right-handed, use your left. This technique is a great one to practise as it encourages you to really look at the object, and can produce interesting results.

Fill the page with butterflies.

82 ———————— Today, try a 'blind' drawing. Find a lamp in your home. Without looking at the paper, draw it. Only peek when you have finished the drawing.

Tip: Draw the outlines of the object, moving your eye (and pencil) slowly around the object. Concentrate on the lines which connect to each other, rather than jumping around on the page.

83 ——— Add the colours, patterns and details to these flowers.

Draw somewhere you have visited.

Add stripes to the bees. Experiment with different mediums, thicknesses and marks.

86

Use the grid to draw geometric shapes. They could be 2D or 3D.

87

Using coloured paper, cut out letters to form a word, name or phrase.

88

Calligraphy practice: try a slow zig-zag today. Press lightly on the upwards stroke, then as you turn down, apply more pressure to form a thicker stroke.

Slowly apply more
pressure here.

Apply just a little
pressure here.

Relieve pressure here to
form a thinner stroke.

89 ——— Colour the rain using different types of art media.

90 ——— Take your time and really look at these leaves, observing their tones and textures. Draw each of the leaves on the next page.

Tip: Perhaps use watercolour paint and allow colours to blend into each other.

91

What activities have you found most challenging so far? Why? How did you overcome the challenge?

92

Colour the grid.

93 ———— Draw a cloud.

94 ———— What made you smile today?

Fill the tree with birds.

Cut a piece of fruit in half and draw what you see.
Use any material you feel like. You could try a variety
of different materials and compare the effects.

Tip: You'll need to work quite quickly, before the fruit turns brown!

Complete the pattern.

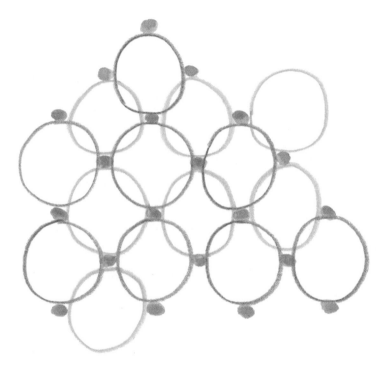

98 ———— Draw lots of noses.

99 ———— Draw the face of someone you have seen today, from memory. Focus on something you specifically remember about them. Perhaps they had interesting shoes or an unusual pair of earrings.

100 ———— Colour in.

101 ——————— Draw some mugs you have in your house.

102 ——————— Draw a tree from your imagination.

103

Using pencils, colour each circle a different shade to create a blend in the middle.

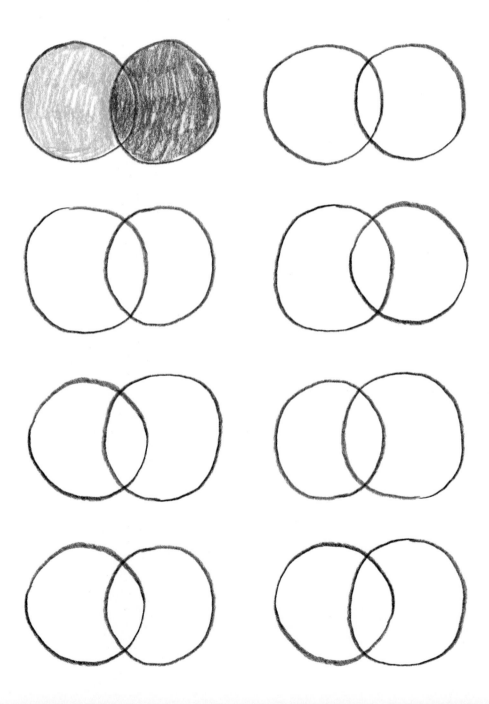

Draw everything you have in your pencil case.

Turn these paint splodges into animals.

106

Draw the horizon on this grey sky. It could be the sea with ships, a headland, a city skyline...

107 ———— Draw lots of mouths.

108 ———— Draw lots of eyes.

109

Add to the reef by drawing your own coral, or by adding fish and sea life.

110 ———————— Design a pattern using the grid.

111 ———

Shading can add depth to your drawings. There are different techniques for shading, including the ones below. Use the right-hand side to try them for yourself.

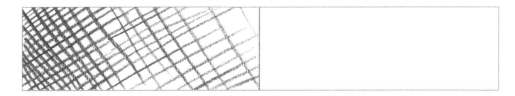

Try cross-hatching. Add more lines to the areas that you'd like to look darker. The denser the area, the darker it appears.

Using a coloured pencil, apply more pressure when shading the areas you'd like to darken. Relieve the pressure to make it lighter.

Use dots to add density to the areas you'd like to be appear darker. The more dots you use, the darker it looks.

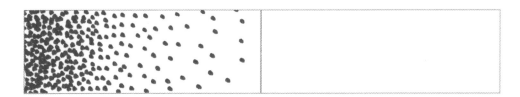

Try watercolour. Start with a light wash of colour, then add more layers of colour in blocks to the areas you'd like to darken.

112 ———— Draw a scene in this window. Are you looking in or out?

113 ———— Draw an animal using cut-out pieces of paper.

Add smiles to these stars.

115 ———— Look outside your window and observe what you see.
Then draw the scene from memory.

116 ———— Write down the top three places you'd like to
visit, and why those places are at the top of
your list.

117

Sometimes when you are on location, trying to choose a subject to draw can be overwhelming. Visit a garden centre or park. Look at plants individually, rather than seeing a scene as a whole. Focus on drawing one plant at a time.

Tip: Don't worry if people look over your shoulder at what you are doing — they are usually very friendly!

118 ———————— Put on some relaxing music, take a coloured pencil
in your hand, close your eyes, then draw as you listen
to the music.

——————— Use this page to paint or draw some skies.

120

Colour in the strawberries using different materials.

Continue the colourful spiral pattern outwards.

122 —————— Today, draw some simple shapes, holding the pencil in the opposite hand to the one you usually use. If you are left-handed, use your right hand. If you are right-handed, use your left. This is a great warm-up exercise for the mind.

123 —————— Draw your favourite part of your home.

124 ——————— Explore different materials to discover what you enjoy using. Today, experiment with collage. Try cutting, tearing and layering the paper.

Draw a wintery forest walk.

Create a design on this rug.

Fill a page with things that are the colour pink.

128 ———————— Design a floral pattern.

Draw something you've never drawn before.

130

Explore colours that look good together. Fill in the boxes
with colours that you think work well as a group.

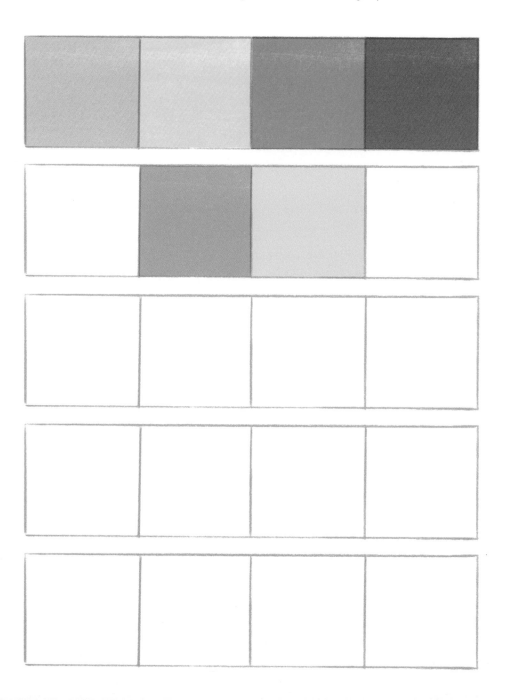

131

Another exercise to try when drawing on location is to draw the negative space around a building, rather than the building itself. Here I have started off by painting the sky around the sky scrapers, and have then added in details such as the windows.

Tip: Take a sketchbook outside and draw what you see, focusing on the negative space around the buildings or trees instead.

Cut a piece of fruit in half and draw what you see. Use any material you feel like. You could try it in a variety of different materials and compare the effects.

Add colour or patterns to the shapes.

134 ———————— Draw someone's smile.

135 ———————— Draw your favourite building.

Using cut-out paper, create a pattern in this section.

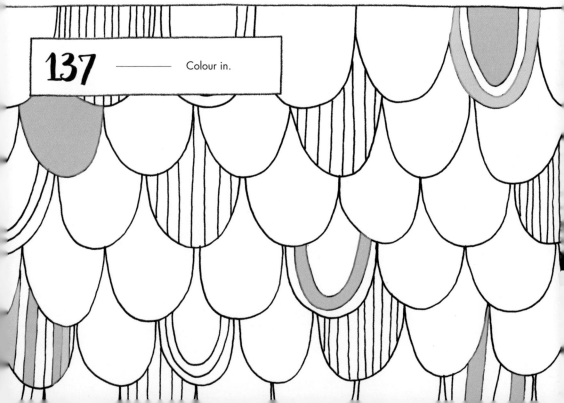

137 Colour in.

Fill the page with colourful beetles.

139

Calligraphy practice: use the brush pen to practise thin to thick strokes by drawing loops. Practise until you feel comfortable making the movement, and can move seamlessly from applying light to harder pressure.

Start with a thin stroke here.

Apply more pressure.

Relieve pressure here, and continue using a thinner line as you move the brush upwards.

Telephone doodle page. Call someone up
for a chat and doodle away!

141 ——————— Observe your reflection and draw what you see.

142 ——————— Draw your favourite animal.

143 ——

Draw each of these leaves on the next page, paying particular attention to the shapes.

Tip: You could use a sharp coloured pencil to draw the outlines.

Colour the leaves using autumnal colours.

145

Draw something outside today, where people might see you. Perhaps on a train or on a bench. It can be as quick as you like, but it's a great way to start building your confidence.

146 —————— Draw or colour the rays of light from the sun.
Perhaps they fill the page.

Add patterns to all the socks.

Draw your home. This could be the front of your house or inside.

149

Fill the page with things that are the colour blue.

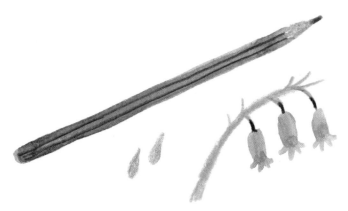

150 ——— Write or draw something you saw or heard today which inspired you, and sparked an idea.

151 ——— Draw a colourful rainbow.

—————— Add the faces.

153

Colour in the shapes.

154

Continue adding coloured zig-zags.

155 —————— Visit a museum or busy train station. Draw the people you
see passing by.

*Tip: Work quickly and don't worry if it's not a masterpiece...
it's more about observing the world around you.*

156

Shading can add depth to your drawings. There are different techniques for shading, including the ones below. Using these four techniques, shade these oranges.

157

Draw the ingredients of your favourite sandwich.

158 ——————— Create some watercolour or paint splodges.
What could they become? A creature? A pattern?

Tip: Use a lot of water on your brush.

159

People watching provides great drawing practice, and can be done whenever you feel like it. Practise drawing people out and about. Take this book, loose paper or a sketchbook onto a train, cafe or anywhere you can sit and look.

Tip: Draw the people you see. Work fast before they move.

160 ———— Add patterns to the butterflies.

Calligraphy practice: use a brush pen to practise 'e'. Apply pressure (by pushing down slightly on the brush) when you make your downwards stroke to create a thicker line. Relieve pressure when bringing the brush up or sideways.

Start applying pressure here.

Start here.

eeeeeeeee

Relieve pressure here.

Fill a page with dads with their children.

Create your own colour wheel by adding in the colours.
The inner layer should show a lighter shade of the outer layer.

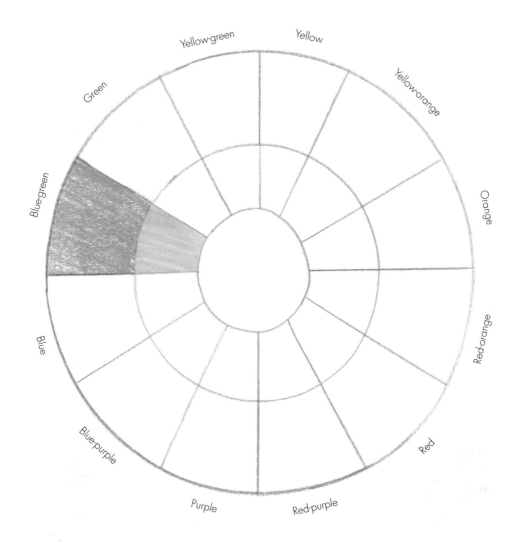

Tip: Complementary colours can be found opposite each other, and these pairs will create striking contrasts within your work. A group of three or more colours next to each other are called analogous, and these will form a harmonious palette when used together.

Use each square to experiment with pattern and mark making.

165 ———— Draw your hand.

166

Draw the leaves blowing off the trees.

167

Sit by an object. (I've chosen a vase of flowers, but choose anything that interests you.) Draw it in four different ways. First, use just a coloured outline, then use blocks of colour, then perhaps try a stylised version. Finally combine all your drawings into a fourth image, choosing elements you like from each of your three initial drawings.

168

Complete a five-minute drawing today. Set a timer, choose an object or a simple scene and spend only five minutes drawing it. Using a pencil, aim to get as much drawn as possible.

Tip: Look at the distances between shapes and think carefully about where you place each line, as every line counts.

169 ——— Add patterns to the bowls.

170 ——————— Draw one thing that made you happy today.

171 ——————— Draw three things you ate today, from memory.

172

Telephone doodle. Call someone up for a chat and doodle away!

173

Fill this quarter with your favourite colour.

174 ———— Find a window in your house where you can sit comfortably and look out. Draw what you see. You could focus on one part of the scene, such as a lamp post or a neighbour's door.

175

Shade the apples in different colours.

176 ——

Calligraphy practice: use a brush pen to practise 'o'. Apply pressure (by pushing down slightly on the brush) when you make your downwards stroke to create a thicker line. Relieve pressure when bringing the brush up or sideways.

Start with downwards stroke here.

Loop round, ready to start a new letter.

(OO OOOOO

Relieve pressure here.

Thin upwards stroke.

177 ———— Design your own fairy (twinkle) lights.

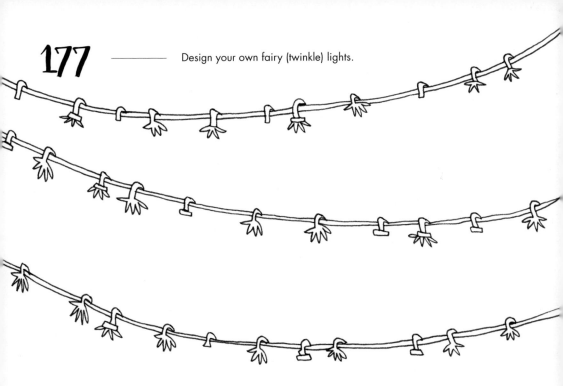

178 ———— Write down five great things that happened to you today.

179

Today, spend 30 minutes drawing. Set a timer, choose an object or scene (perhaps the corner of a room) and spend 30 minutes observing and drawing it. Try using colour and look carefully before you draw. As you have a more sustained period of time to draw, you have time to consider where you apply colour and line.

Design the houses in the streets.

181 —————— Draw someone important to you.

182 —————— Draw your favourite pair of shoes.

183 —————— Create an image using the grid. An abstract scene?
A shape?

Draw some of the items you have in your store cupboard.

185 ———— Draw your breakfast using blocks of colour. Having it in front of you will encourage you to work quickly!

Tip: You could apply colour with cut-out pieces of paper, large washes of paint, or using coloured pencils.

Create a page of cats.

187

Explore different materials to discover what you enjoy using. Today, try a brush pen to create different marks. You can use the brush at different angles, and apply different pressures, to vary the effects.

188 ———— Write down a positive phrase or mantra.

189 ———— Draw the weather today.

190 ——————— Colour in.

191 ——————— Who inspires you at the moment? Why?

192 ———— Colour in the circles to create a rainbow gradient going down the page. Fill the top row with dark blue, the next row with turquoise, and so on. Try to use different materials like paint, paper from magazines, and coloured paper.

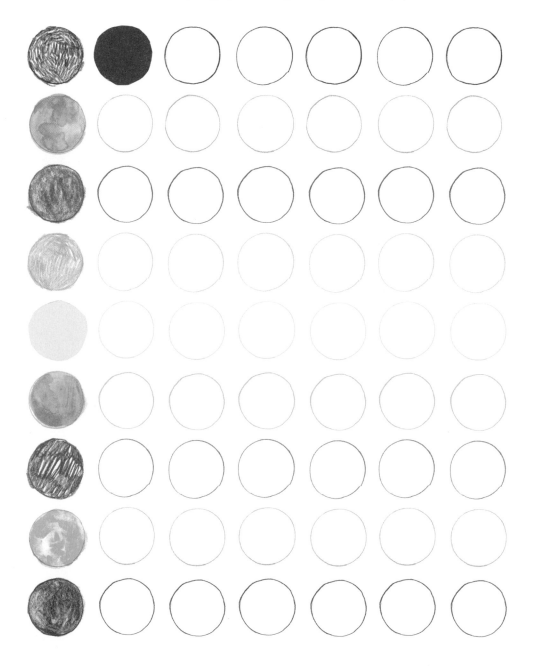

193

Fill a page with things that are the colour green.

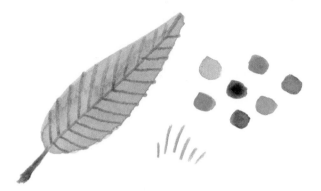

194 ——————— Remember a time when somebody made a positive remark about your creativity. Write it down here.

195 ——————— What are you proud of this week?

196 ——————— Draw a fictional character.

197 ——————— Fill this quarter of the page with coloured dots.

Use the page opposite to create your own repeating pattern using simple drawings of objects or shapes.

1. Draw a simple object.

2. Repeatedly draw the object, keeping an even space between the drawings. Each drawing does not need to be perfect at all – in fact, it is the handmade, unique effect that will give your pattern charm.

3. Add in more elements if needed.

199

Colour in the pebbles. Try to experiment with shading and texture.

200

Experiment with different materials to discover what you enjoy using. Today, try watercolour paints to create different marks. You could try varying the brush size, angle of the brush, and how much water you use.

Tip: Watercolours are great for blending colours. Experiment with this by applying two colours next to each other on the page, and allow the colours to run into each other.

201

Choose six or seven pencils in a range of colours. Look around you and draw the objects that you see as a line drawing, using a different colour for each object. Only draw the outlines, rather than adding shaded areas. Explore layering your drawings over each other and you will create a colourful, energetic interpretation of what you see around you – don't worry about accuracy.

202

Explore colours that look good together. Fill in the boxes with colours that you think work well as a set.

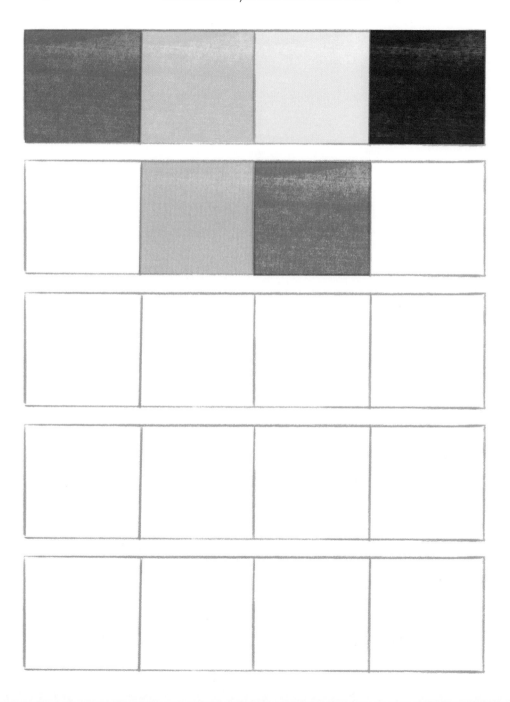

203 ———————— For this activity, focus only on negative space, which is the shape you see around an object. Draw someone's profile (the side of their face) using just the negative space. You don't have to colour it in black. You could try using a pattern or lots of different colours. Try it on the opposite page.

Tip: You could use a photograph or draw from real life. To draw the negative space you will need to look at the shapes and angles around an object, rather than the object itself. This teaches us to look, and working in this way helps us to understand how to draw an object itself.

204 ———————— Challenge yourself today. Draw something you struggle with. Tackle it by simplifying it. Perhaps focus on the block shapes and key features rather than an outline.

Add plants to the pots.

206 ———— Fill this section with smiley faces.

207 ———— Draw an object using coloured pencils or pastels. Use this coloured background as a mid-tone. Use light colours to draw the highlights and darker colours to draw the shadows.

208 ———— Write or draw something you saw or heard today
which inspired you, and sparked an idea.

209 ———— Colour in.

Design the pattern on
the lampshade.

211

Calligraphy practice: this time, use a brush pen to practice 'a'.

Start with downwards stroke here.

Once at the top, bring the brush down using a full stroke.

Thin upwards stroke.

212 ————— Continue the trompe-l'œil drawing to create an optical illusion. Use a brush pen, and vary the widths of the lines to trick your eye into seeing a 3D form.

213 ————— Experiment with the 'resist' technique. First, draw a pattern with pastels (which are oil-based) then paint over the top with watercolour. As oil and water don't mix, the oil pastel will repel the watercolour.

——————— Add in the stormy sea.

215

Today, try using pencils to create different marks. Experiment by using the side of the lead to create broader lines.

216 ——————— On a dark, clear night, go outside and draw the stars. Use white pencil on this black background to draw your constellations.

217

Visit a park or garden and observe the people interacting with the plants. Try drawing or painting quickly and loosely and don't worry too much about accuracy. It's the character you are after!

218 ———————— What have you enjoyed drawing so far?

219 ———————— Colour in the concentric circles. These could be shades of different colours such as green or yellow.

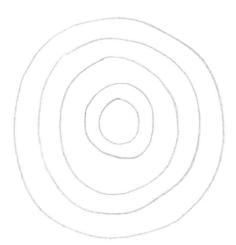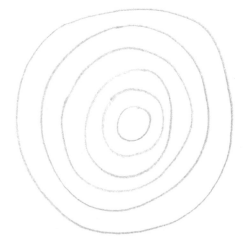

Turn these paint splodges into vases of flowers.

221 ————— Design a pattern which reminds you of a summery beach.

222 ————— Draw the ingredients in your favourite recipe.

Use each square to experiment with pattern and mark making.

First, choose an object to draw. Practise drawing it with both hands at once: hold a pencil in each hand and, starting at the top of the object, draw simultaneously using both pencils. Use the left side of the page to draw the left side of the object with your left hand, and the right side of the page to draw the right side of the object with your right hand!

Tip: Keep both pencils moving at the same time, as your eyes flick from the left to the right of the object. It might be easier to concentrate on looking at the object, rather than the page you are drawing on.

225

Fill the tree with autumn (fall) leaves.

226 ———— What did you love to draw when you were a child? Draw or write it here.

_____

_____

_____

_____

_____

227 ———— Draw some hairstyles which you observed today, from memory.

228 ———— What activities are you most proud of so far? Why?

229 ———— Today, share some of your artwork with someone. This could be online, or in real life. Ask them what they like about your artwork. Write what they say here.

Explore colours that look good together. Fill in the boxes with colours that you think work well as a group.

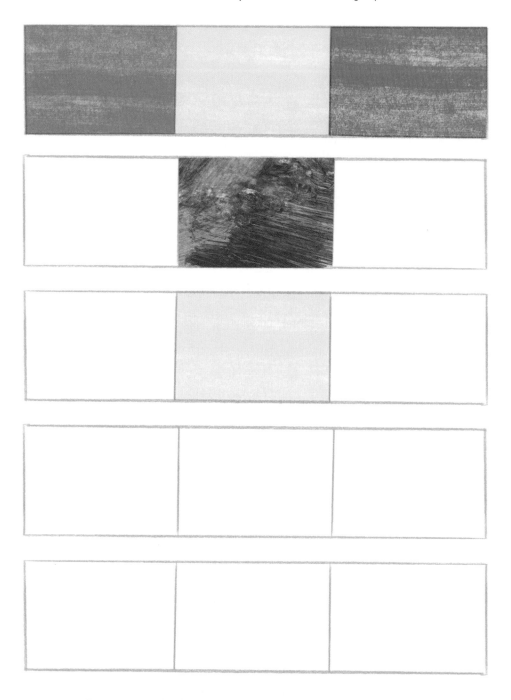

231

Colour in between the wavy lines.

232

Add coloured patterns to the waves. Consider using a chalky white pencil to add to the darker colours.

233 ——————

Calligraphy practice: use a brush pen to practise 's'. This letter can be tricky, but just keep in mind to apply more pressure on downward strokes, and less pressure when moving up.

Bring the brush down and around using a full stroke.

Start with a thin stroke here.

Relieve pressure here and as you move up, use a very light, thin stroke.

Fill the page with pebbles.

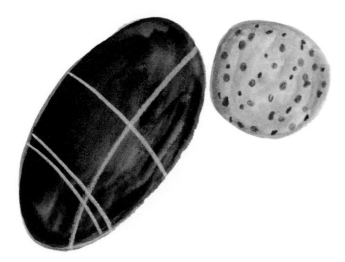

235

Today, try using a black fineliner pen to create different marks. Try different nib sizes for varying thickness of line.

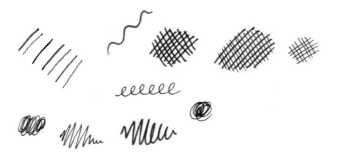

Draw your five favourite fruit. Think about how you position them on the page. Are they in a group, or displayed separately? Are they whole or have they been half-eaten?

237 ———— Colour in.

238

Try monoprinting with oil pastels. (This can get messy, so you might like to try on another piece of paper first.) Start by finding a clean sheet of thin paper. Use a coloured pastel to cover an area on the sheet of paper with colour. Lay this, coloured side down, on another piece of paper, then carefully draw with a sharp pencil on the back of the coloured paper. See how the coloured pastel transfers to the new piece of paper in the areas where you draw. Experiment with this process.

Here, I have used a red pastel to cover the first piece of paper. When using the pencil to transfer your drawing, you can press harder to create a darker, more definite line, as done here on the outside of the flower.

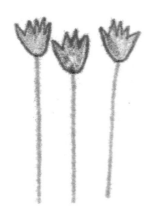

You could try experimenting with multiple colours. Just use a new thin sheet of paper to lay down a new colour using pastel. It's tricky to see exactly where you are transferring second colour in relation to the first, but that is part of the fun!

239 ———— Write something that happened today that made you feel proud.

240 ———— Arrange some small objects in front of you. Draw the negative space around them.

241

Draw an animal from life. Animals are great subjects as they don't mind being drawn! They do tend to move around a lot, so practise working quickly, and try to draw the key information and characteristics.

242 ———— Make a pattern in the shapes.

243 ——————— Draw the cover of your favourite book.

Add patterns to the shells.

Draw somewhere you would like to visit.

246 ———— Draw some cutlery.

247 ———— Try a continuous drawing outside. Visit a park or beach and draw what you see in front of you without lifting your pencil from the page. This will encourage you to consider the relationship and distances between objects in front of you.

248 ———— Draw some people.

249 ———— What are you looking forward to tomorrow?

250 ———— Who or what has made you laugh this week?

251 ———— Fill this section with geometric shapes.

252

Today, create a drawing using one continuous pencil line. Choose an object, and draw the outline without taking your pencil off the page (unless you really need to). This activity helps to co-ordinate what your eye sees and what your pencil does.

Tip: Try your own on the next page. You may need to double back on your line to continue the drawing.

253

Add in the horizon, or the rooftops of the buildings you can see.

Colour in the boats, and give each of them a name.

255 ———————— Practise people watching. Use pencil and work quickly, trying to capture the personality of the person in your drawing.

256 ———————— Look at the previous drawing and redraw the elements you like, adding colour.

257

Explore different materials to discover what you enjoy using. Today, experiment with oil pastels to create different marks. You can try smudging them with your finger to blend colours.

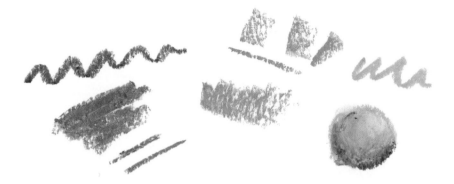

Tip: Oil pastels can produce fun results, but are also messy. To protect the opposite page, you could attach a layer of tracing paper to this page once you have finished.

258 ———— Use the grid to design a pattern.

Design the pattern on the fan.

260 ———————— Sit in front of a mirror and draw yourself.

261

Here are some shelves. Draw your favourite books.
You could show the cover or the spines.

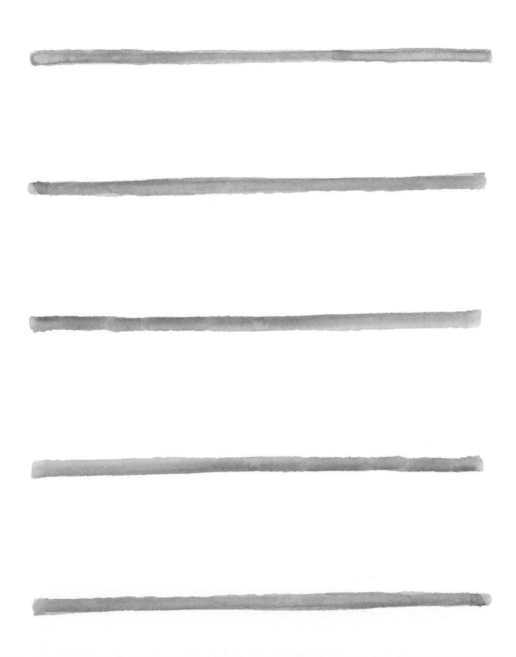

262 ——————— Write the names of some of the people who make you happy. Perhaps sketch their faces. It can be as simple as you like.

263 ——————— What inspired you today?

Calligraphy practice: today, draw 'f'. Enjoy its loopy shape.

Bring the brush down using a full stroke.

Start with a thin stroke here.

Relieve pressure here to form a thinner stroke.

265 ———— Find a tree. Study the bark of the tree and draw the wood grain.

266 ———— Draw a bird from your imagination.

267

Fill the harbour with boats.

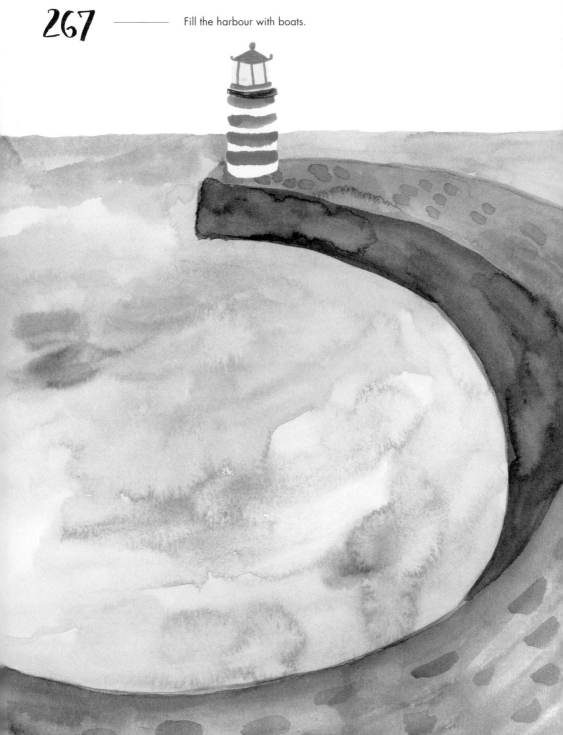

268 ———— The rule of thirds is a handy trick used to help compositions to look visually attractive. Here, the page is divided into thirds. Create a drawing using these sections as a guide, placing elements into some of the thirds, perhaps one or two thirds, rather than in the centre.

269

Today, try drawing with a line and wash. Use a fineliner pen or sharp pencil to draw something. Then, add colour and tone to your drawing using a watercolour wash.

1.

2.

270

Fill the page with pattern.

271

Find an image of your favourite piece of artwork. Create your own version of it below. Use materials that feel natural to you.

When drawing outside, or 'on location', you don't need to draw everything you see in front of you. Instead, you could try just drawing the areas that interest you the most. In this drawing, I enjoyed looking at all the features on the rooftops.

Tip: Take this book outside, choose a building or scene and look at it for a while. What specifically interests you about the scene? What would you like to explore through your drawing? Focus on those areas.

273 ————— Draw an urban landscape. Perhaps pick something you wouldn't usually choose to draw.

Fill a page with things that are the colour purple.

Calligraphy practice: today, use the opposite page to try an alphabet. Join letters where it feels natural to do so. There is no right or wrong way to do this, as your calligraphy will always have personality, and isn't at all about perfection.

abcdefgh
ijklmnop
qrstuv
wxyz

276 ———— Using coloured pencils, write down something that inspired you this month.

277 ———— Call up a friend. Ask them, 'What is your favourite animal?' Draw it!

Add plants to the pots.

279 ———— Cut a piece of fruit in half and draw what you see. Use any material you feel like. You could try a variety of different materials and compare the effects.

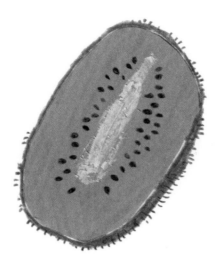

Colour in the circles.

281 ————— Complete a one-minute drawing today. Set a timer, choose an object and spend a minute drawing it. Using a pencil, aim to get as much of the object drawn as possible. Working with short time limits encourages you to draw without having to worry about whether the lines you make are wrong or right.

What is in the jars? Pickles? Fruit? Insects? What would you store in these jars?

283 ——————— Colour in.

284

Using a big paint brush, fill the page with painted strokes.

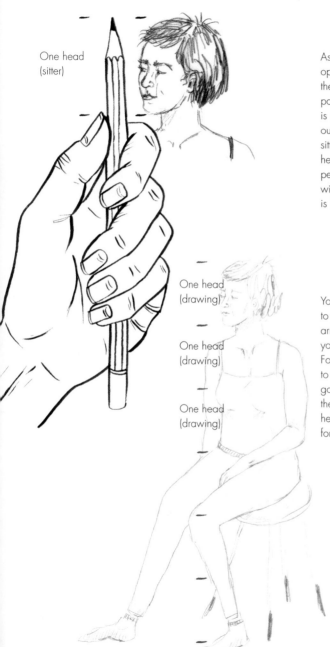

One head
(sitter)

One head
(drawing)

One head
(drawing)

One head
(drawing)

Ask someone to sit for you, and use the opposite page for your drawing. First, draw their head, leaving plenty of space on the page for the rest of the body. Once the head is drawn, hold your pencil and arm straight out in front of you in the direction of your sitter. Close one eye, look at the person's head and move your thumb down your pencil until the top of your thumb is level with their chin, and the top of the pencil is level with the top of their head.

You can then use this 'one head' measurement to plot the rest of the body. Still holding out your arm, measure the rest of the body, keeping your thumb fixed on the 'one head' distance. For example, the distance from the shoulders to the hips may be 'two heads'. You can then go back to your drawing, and check that the distance from the shoulder to the hips is the height of two of your drawn heads. And so on for the rest of the body.

Choose an object or see if someone will sit still for you. Take a pencil in both your left and right hands. Start looking at and drawing the object (or person), keeping both pencils moving at the same time. The left hand should work down the left side of the object, and the right hand down the right side. This is a great exercise for your brain!

287

Add in the sky, sea and beach. Perhaps there are people on the beach.

Create a page of fields. What could be in them?

289

Explore colours that look good together. Fill in the boxes with colours that you think work well side by side.

Fill a page with things that are the colour orange.

Add details to the leaves.

292 ——————— Blind drawings teach us to see as well as just look. Draw someone without looking at your page. Just look closely at their face and the shapes and angles. It may not be pretty, but it's great practice. Use the opposite page to create your blind portrait.

Use this page to paint or draw some skies.

Experiment with shading to colour in these pears.
Try using the pencils in different ways. Be playful.

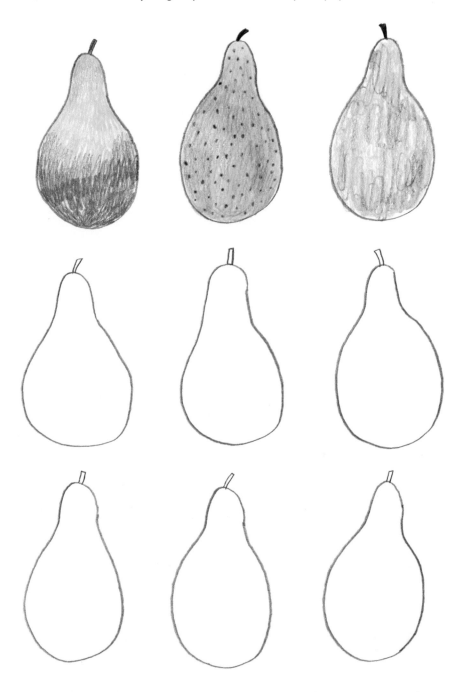

295

For this drawing, choose another object or scene, and use a continuous pencil line for each separate colour that you see. Only take the pencil off the page when you must. This technique can lead to some interesting results. Try your own on the next page.

Fill the wheel with colour using watercolours. Consider which colours may look appealing next to each other.

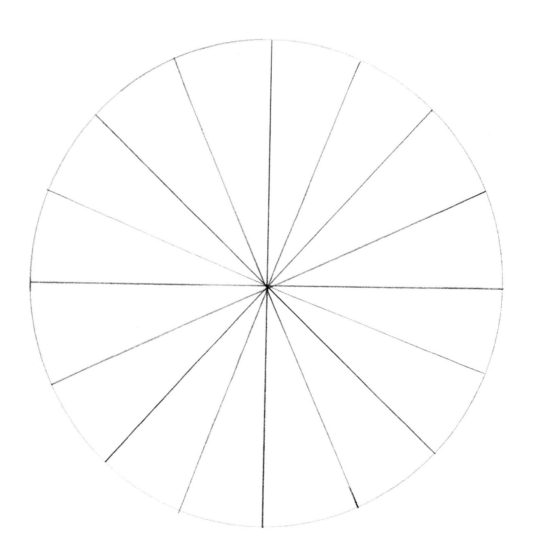

297

Today, create a drawing which shows perspective. Using the grey lines as a guide, draw a row of trees. Your trees don't need to fit into the lines exactly, but the lines can be used to show roughly how big objects of similar height may appear. Perhaps add extra plants and people once you've finished.

298

Explore mark making using charcoal and an eraser. Start by turning a charcoal stick on its side and rubbing it over the paper. Then use erasers to remove material and create white marks. See what effects you can create in the space below.

Tip: You may want to tape a sheet of tracing paper over your drawing once you've finished, as it can get a bit messy!

299 ———— Create an abstract garden. You could use cut-out pieces of paper or any other material. Start by drawing plants, and keep adding layers. You could add vegetables, animals and birds.

What are the people looking at? Draw it.

301 ———— Draw a dense, tropical forest with palm trees and exotic flowers.

302 ——————— Draw an object so that it fills the whole page.

303 ———— Add rain to this grey sky. Think about how you could represent the raindrops. Are they lines? Individual dots?

304 ———— Draw a bowl of food.

305 ———— Create a pattern using a black fineliner pen.

306 ———————— Continue the pattern until the page is filled.

307

Cut or tear strips of coloured paper and use them to create your own abstract sea image on the opposite page. Is it a calm or choppy sea?

Tip: You could draw onto the paper first using coloured pencils.

Calligraphy practice: use the opposite page to try numbers. The same principles apply as when you are drawing letters. Use the full stroke, with more pressure, on the downwards stroke, and the thin line on upwards strokes.

1 2 3

4 5 6 7

8 9 0

309 ———— Draw or doodle within the grid lines.

Fill the page with pebbles.

311

Spend some time shading today. Using the techniques you have learned, shade this colourful vase.

Design patterns for the jumpers (sweaters).

313 —————— Draw a map of a journey you have recently taken.

314 ——— Design a tile.

315

Use this rough guide to draw a face in profile. Most often, the eyes are halfway between the top of the head and the chin. Study the side of somebody's face. Notice where the eye, ear and hairline are. Add in eyebrows too, and the shape of the nose and lips.

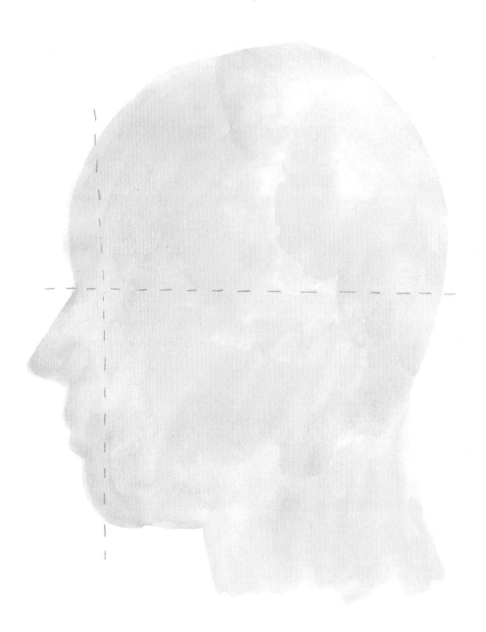

316 ———— Draw a night-time scene outside this window.

317 ———— Glue in an article that interests you.

318

Continue to build your confidence with your art. Draw something in public today, where people might see you. Perhaps in a cafe. It can be as quick as you like and it's a great way to make you feel more comfortable drawing.

319

Use cut-out pieces of paper to draw some plants. You could use coloured pencils to add details. If you would like a particular shade, you could paint over some white paper. Be sure to let it dry before cutting.

320

Calligraphy practice: try writing your name using the skills you have practised.

321 ———— Put on some fast-paced music, take a coloured pencil in your hand, close your eyes and draw as you listen to the music.

322

Today, try drawing with a line and wash. This time, create your wash first, by roughly painting an object in watercolor. Then use a fineliner pen or sharp coloured pencil to add detail and outline.

1.

2.

323

Draw a landscape under this sky.

324 ——————— Complete a drawing while you are out and about.
Draw something that interests you during your day.

Tip: Have a pencil case of materials ready in your bag. Some black fineliner pens, pencils and coloured pencils might be all you need.

325 —————— Draw a page of mums with their children.

—————— Colour in.

327

Observe faces, looking carefully at the position of the eyes, which are usually halfway down. Draw as many as you can here.

328 ———————— Draw some methods of transport.

329 ——————— Draw the individual items in your favourite outfit.

Add flowers to the stalks.

331 ——————— Using the calligraphy skills you have learned, write your name below.

332 ——————— Build your confidence by sharing your work. Create a piece of work (it can be as big or small as you like) and share it with anyone. Perhaps a friend, or family member, or even on social media.

Tip: Showing people what you've created can be scary, but it can be surprisingly rewarding. Try it!

333 ———— Using watercolours, paint something you remember from your day.

334

Turn this paint stroke into a house. You could use white as a highlight.

335

Draw your coloured pencils and then colour them in.

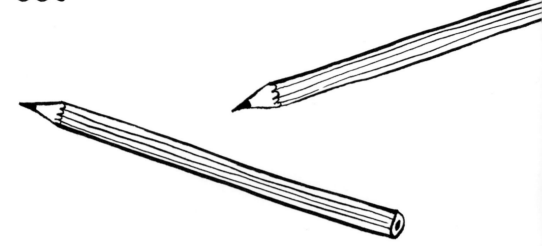

336 ——— Using white pastel or a chalky white coloured pencil, draw on the black areas.

337 ———— Draw an object as small as you possibly can.
You may need a very fine pen or sharp pencil.

338 ———— Draw something you remember seeing today.

339 ———— Write down a time when someone made a positive comment about your creativity.

340 ———— Draw a pair of shoes which you observed today.

—————— Continue the pattern until the page is filled.

342 ———— What made you smile today?

343 ———— Draw lots of ears.

344

Explore using charcoal and a rubber to draw an image. Cover the page with charcoal and choose a subject. Use the rubber to remove charcoal from the page. Sometimes it helps to roughly mark areas you'd like to lighten using your thumb, as this removes some of the charcoal too. Focus on areas of highlight.

Tip: You can then use a charcoal stick to add in darker areas and detail to your drawing. You may like to protect your drawing when finished, by taping a sheet of tracing paper over it.

345 ——— What are the people looking at? Draw it.

346 ———— What has inspired you this week?

347 ———— Using the calligraphy skills you have learned, write the name of someone close to you.

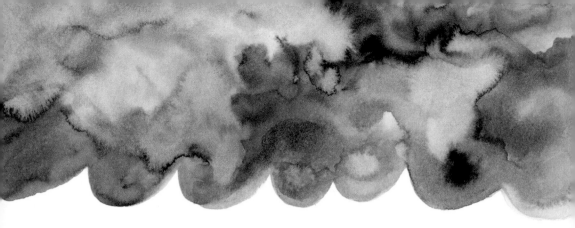

348 —— Draw under the waves.

349 ———— Use charcoal and an eraser to draw a face. You could work from a photograph or real life. Start by laying down a base of charcoal by turning it on its side and covering the page. This will be your mid-tone. Then use the eraser to draw the highlights in the face. Finally, add in the detail and darker areas using a charcoal stick.

Colour in.

351 ———— Coloured paper can be used as a mid-tone for a drawing. Use pastels or coloured pencils and explore using bright colours to add highlights and shadow to your drawings.

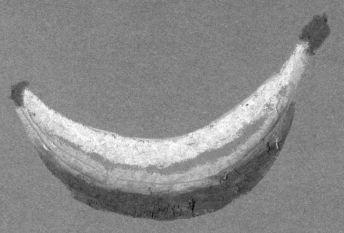

352

Today, create a line drawing of a simple scene. Arrange a few objects in front of you, and draw the outlines. Sometimes it's helpful to close one eye as you look at the scene. Concentrate on the distance and angles between the objects.

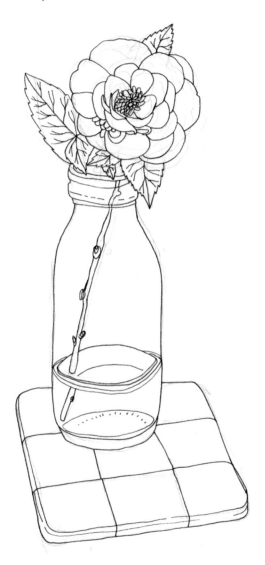

Tip: You could draw the scene in pencil first, using this to work out where everything is placed. It can then be erased when you've drawn over it in pen.

353

Practise drawing the features of a face on the opposite page.
Draw the eyes about halfway down the face, and the bottom of
the nose on the nose line. Perhaps find a photo of a face to study.

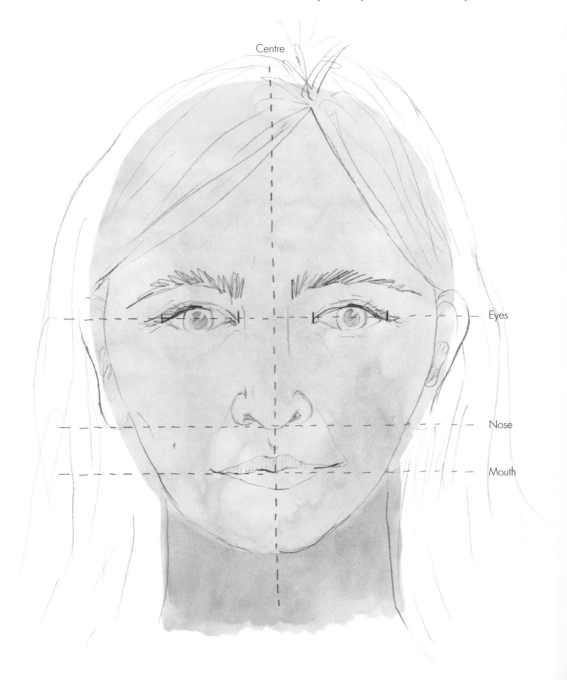

Centre

Eyes

Nose

Mouth

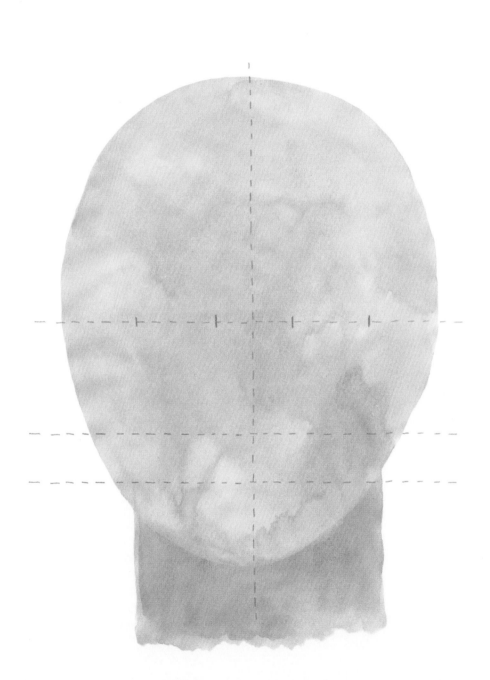

354 ———— Draw your feet.

355 ———— Write a stream of conciousness. Just write what comes into your mind. There's no need to read it back.

356

Decorate the circles with patterns.

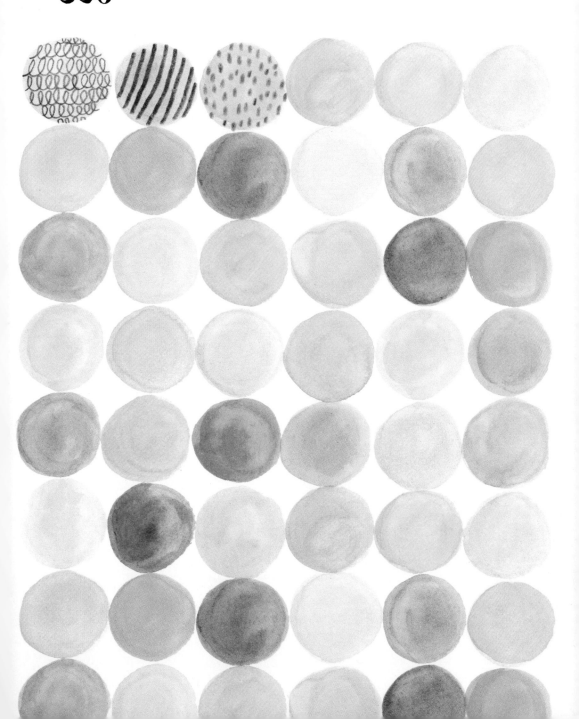

357

Today, create a drawing which shows perspective. Use the grey lines as guides to draw a row of houses. The grey dot where the lines meet on the horizon is called the 'vanishing point'. By drawing objects of a similar size (like a row of houses) within these lines, they will appear to get further away until they reach the vanishing point.

Vanishing Point.

Tip: The angles and lines within your drawing don't have to be perfect. As long as you roughly follow the grey lines as a base to your drawing, it should still give the effect of objects getting further away. Perhaps add people to the street, or a pavement.

358 ———— Draw what the paint brush has painted.

359

Colour in the forest.

360

Draw a scene, but instead of drawing the objects themselves, focus on the negative space around them. You may want to very roughly draw your composition in pencil first, but really concentrate on the space and angles around your objects. Look at shapes in between lines rather than lines themselves.

Tip: You could use any material you like for this drawing. Here I've used coloured pencil; if you choose to do the same, it's helpful to keep your pencil nice and sharp.

361

Draw the horizon beneath this sunset. It could be the sea
with ships, a headland, a city skyline...

362 ———— Add patterns to the scarves.

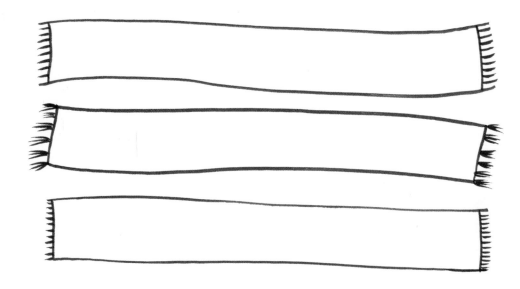

363 ———— Create a collage of coloured paper. You could paint the paper first and then cut it into shapes once it has dried.

364 ——————— Create an abstract jungle. You could use cut-out pieces of paper or any other material. Start by drawing plants, and keep adding layers to your jungle to give it depth.

365

Calligraphy practice: try writing a friend's name using the skills you have practised. Perhaps you could then send them a handwritten letter or card. Their postal address on the envelope is another great place to show off your calligraphy skills.

About the Author

Lorna Scobie grew up in the depths of the English countryside, climbing trees and taking her rabbit for walks in the fields. She is an illustrator and designer, now based in south London. Growing up surrounded by nature has heavily influenced her illustrations and her work almost always revolves around the natural world and animal kingdom.

Lorna draws every day, and always has a sketchbook close to hand when she's out and about, just in case. She illustrates her work by hand rather than digitally, as she enjoys the spontaneity and also the 'happy mistakes' that can happen along the way. Her favourite places to draw are museums and botanical gardens.

If you'd like to keep up to date with Lorna's work, she can be found on Instagram and Twitter: **@lornascobie**

Thank you

To my editor Kajal, for her unwavering support. Thank you also to my mum Emily, my brother Felix and my partner Joseph for their ears and ideas.

365 Days of Art by Lorna Scobie

First published in 2017 by Hardie Grant Books, an imprint of Hardie Grant Publishing

Hardie Grant Books (UK)
52-54 Southwark Street
London SE1 1UN

Hardie Grant Books (Australia)
Ground Floor, Building 1
658 Church Street
Melbourne, VIC 3121

hardiegrantbooks.com

British Library Cataloguing-in-Publication Data. A catalogue record
for this book is available from the British Library.

ISBN: 978-1-78488-111-5

Publisher: Kate Pollard
Senior Editor: Kajal Mistry
Editorial Assistant: Hannah Roberts
Publishing Assistant: Eila Purvis
Art Direction: Studio Noel
Colour Reproduction by p2d

Printed and bound in China by Leo Paper Group